Be Gentle with Love

Celestial Arts,

Be Gentle with Love

Donni Betts

231 Adrian Road, Millbrae, California 94030

Copyright © 1978 by Celestial Arts

Celestial Arts
231 Adrian Road
Millbrae, California 94030

First Printing, June 1978

Made in the United States of America

Photo: Maria Demarest
Cover Design: Masako Yoshimura
Interior Design: Robert Hu

Library of Congress Cataloging in Publication Data

Betts, Donni.
    Be gentle with love.

    1. Love poetry, American.   I. Title.
PS3552.E83B4   811'.5'4   78-54475
ISBN 0-89087-229-5

1   2   3   4   5   6   7   —   84   83   82   81   80   79   78

for George

Be gentle with love
    as with a newly opened flower,
for love can be fragile.
But if treated with care
and nourished with tenderness,
nature will take her course
    and love will blossom . . .

When we first met
you seemed shy, unsure,
   unwilling to trust yourself,
      afraid of your own emotions.
You tried to cover your insecurities
with a laugh
   and a lightheartedness that
      couldn't conceal your pain.

Gradually, as you began
   to discover
   that people love you
      in spite of your fears,
         you began to shed them.
You are developing the security
   to see that
      the beauty you possess
      is strong enough
         to carry you through life
as you really are.

For today,
let me be a girl
*   of sixteen again,*
and you my first,
*   innocent love.*

Just this once
*   let's recapture the thrill*
*   of a golden summer day,*
*   a gentle kiss,*
and let me remember once again
the first time I saw
*   that look in your eyes,*
*   meant only for me.*

Or has that time
   already passed us by,
never to be known again,
except perhaps
   in tender memory?

I'm not sad
   to see it go . . .
We've replaced it
   with something even more beautiful,
      more enduring . . .
         our love.

But isn't it sweet to dream . . .

I see your shell,
fragile,
     protecting you from hurt.
yet limiting you
     from involvement.

At times the shell slips
and I see glimpses
     of the beautiful,
     warm and fragile
          creature within,
wanting to be loved
     and yet afraid
          of being hurt.

I want you to know
     that I see your warmth
     and beauty,
     your unselfish,
          giving nature
and I hope you know
that you deserve to be loved,
and that you're beautiful
          without your shell.

What do you do
  when your life
    is falling apart?
What can you say
  to turn back the time
    to a happier place?
What do you do
  with the loneliness
    that has been
    a stranger
      for so long?
How can you give
  when all that's there
    is emptiness
    and pain . . .

Frustration . . .
    incompletion . . .
Why?
    You helped create it
        and now you're asleep,
            safe,
and I feel alone
    with my frustration.
What do I do with it?

I can't talk
    with no one to listen.
Maybe you're right . . .
    maybe sleep is the answer
for those who can . . .
            I can't.

We shared something fleeting,
something that time
can neither add to
  nor take from . . .
a feeling of understanding.

I felt it
  and I sense that
    you did too.
I wanted you to know
  I care
and I couldn't say goodbye
    without telling you.

When finally I have
the strength to cry for me
I have the strength
to acknowledge
my own weaknesses,
and from there . . .

Your life is a gift
  for you give of yourself
    to everyone you meet.

Please be with me
when I cry,
when I'm down,
when I'm hurting.
I know it's hard for you,
that you get tired of it.
but that's what
loving is about . . .
sharing the hard times
as well as the good times.
I need you now
more than ever.
And you know
I'll be with you
when it's your turn to cry.

So good to find you again,
                    friend.
after so many years,
and to find you
    happy with life,
    at peace with yourself
    and content in your new love.

No longer straining, pulling,
    and full of an ache
for something you
    didn't even know
        you wanted.

Our paths cross
    and once again
I am filled with happiness
and so glad
    you are still a part
    of my life,
as well as my memory
            of the past.
Welcome back, my special friend . . .

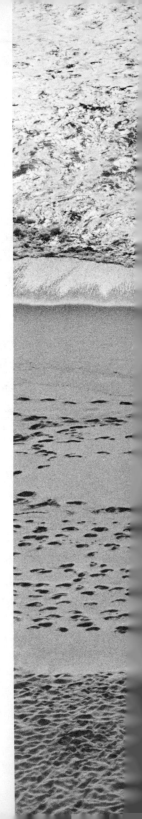

They lie on the beach
  almost touching,
spreading oil over their
  white bodies,
hoping the sun
  will take away
the emptiness grown
in their hearts from too many
years spent together
  without appreciation.
The long awaited vacation
    has arrived
and with it a quiet determination
for change, newness
and excitement in their life together.
When they leave
they'll take their
  temporarily darkened bodies
  and one more week of memories
    to be put away
and remembered only in the
    deepest moments of loneliness.

It's the not knowing
      that's hard to take,
not knowing how you feel.
It's beginning to get me down.

Have I invaded a part
            of your life
      that isn't meant for me?
Am I coming too close
      to feelings that
         you had reserved
               for only you?

It's just not knowing
      that's so hard
         to live with.
So what do I do?
Continue to wonder,
      or take a risk
      and ask you?

You've exposed yourself,
naked somehow,
   a soul
     alone.

You became frightened,
overwhelmed by feelings
   you didn't realize
     you possessed.

Then you return to a safe place
inside
where you don't have
   to reveal anything.

I am still
   waiting,
wondering if you know
how beautiful
   you are when you are
     naked.

*Funny, I never realized
how silent our home is
    when you're away.*

*But even in the quiet
    I feel
        the comfort
    of your presence.*

*Your gentleness will carry
    me to sleep tonight
        as it has every night.*

*Good night . . .
    Sleep well . . .*

I cry out
    but no one listens.
I try to speak
    but you turn away.
I feel so alone.
Won't someone help me
    break out of my shell
and learn to cry,
            to feel?
Help me back into the world?
Doesn't anyone care about me?
I need you . . .

I can't imagine life
*   without you . . .*
What has happened to us
*   to bring such*
*   emptiness and heartache?*
How did we manage
*   to drift so far apart?*
Was it because we were
*   too close?*

Where have you gone that I can't see you?

What did you want that I could not give?

I see it so clearly now,
  things I've felt for awhile
    but couldn't put into words.
It's not that we've lost anything,
  yet something is slipping
              away from us.
I've seen glimpses of it.
            here and there . . .
    too involved with
      a hurry-up world,
      a job,
          a friend,
not taking enough time
    to really care.
We can still recapture
what we're missing
if we will only take time . . .

Everyone comes to you
   with their burdens
        and problems.
I know it can be fulfilling
   but it can drain your spirit
        as well.
Where do you go with your burdens?

Come, love, and I will hold you,
   in silence,
        and help you pass off your
        burdens,
           quietly.
I'll try to understand.

When you left today
  I felt afraid,
    I didn't want you to go.
I wanted you to stay
  and reassure me
    I'd see you tomorrow
    or soon . . .

But the look in your eyes
    told me not to say
      the things I felt,
that you were in a hurry
    to get back to your world.
I know I'll see you again,
    but will the closeness
      still be there,
or have you already
    moved on
    leaving me alone
      with the feelings
        we once shared?

When I was young
I loved things
like dolls
   and kittens.
As I grew older
   my love grew
   to encompass
      joyous moments
         with people,
            with nature.

How can I tell you
how full my life is
becoming
   since you?
Our love is becoming
               a key,
opening doors
   to many of
      the joys of life
         we would never
have discovered
               alone.

I have found a few
*   true friends*
as I've traveled
*   throughout life.*
Your friendship is one
I'll carry with me,
*   wherever I go . . .*

I was childish today,
crying foolishly
over something that
didn't really matter.
And you were patient with me
as with a difficult child,
searching beyond your own needs
for a way to comfort me
and take away the hurt.

I knew I was being selfish
but I needed something,
reassurance maybe,
and just the fact that you
could understand
and not withdraw in anger
made it all right again.

After all this time
I still need to be reminded
that you love me
even in my weakest,
most vulnerable moments . . .

I'm waiting
for spring to arrive.
For newness,
    green
        freshness
    to burst into our lives
and banish the heavy,
    cloud-days of winter.

Already I can feel
the sunshine
    brought by blooming
        daffodils,
    the first perfumed hint
    of new-mown grass
and the sense of endless freedom
    that warm, cloudless
        days promise.

The sun is hidden now
behind a blanket
    of heavy white flakes
and yet I feel
    the airiness of spring
        welling inside me,
        warming me already.
It won't be long now . . .

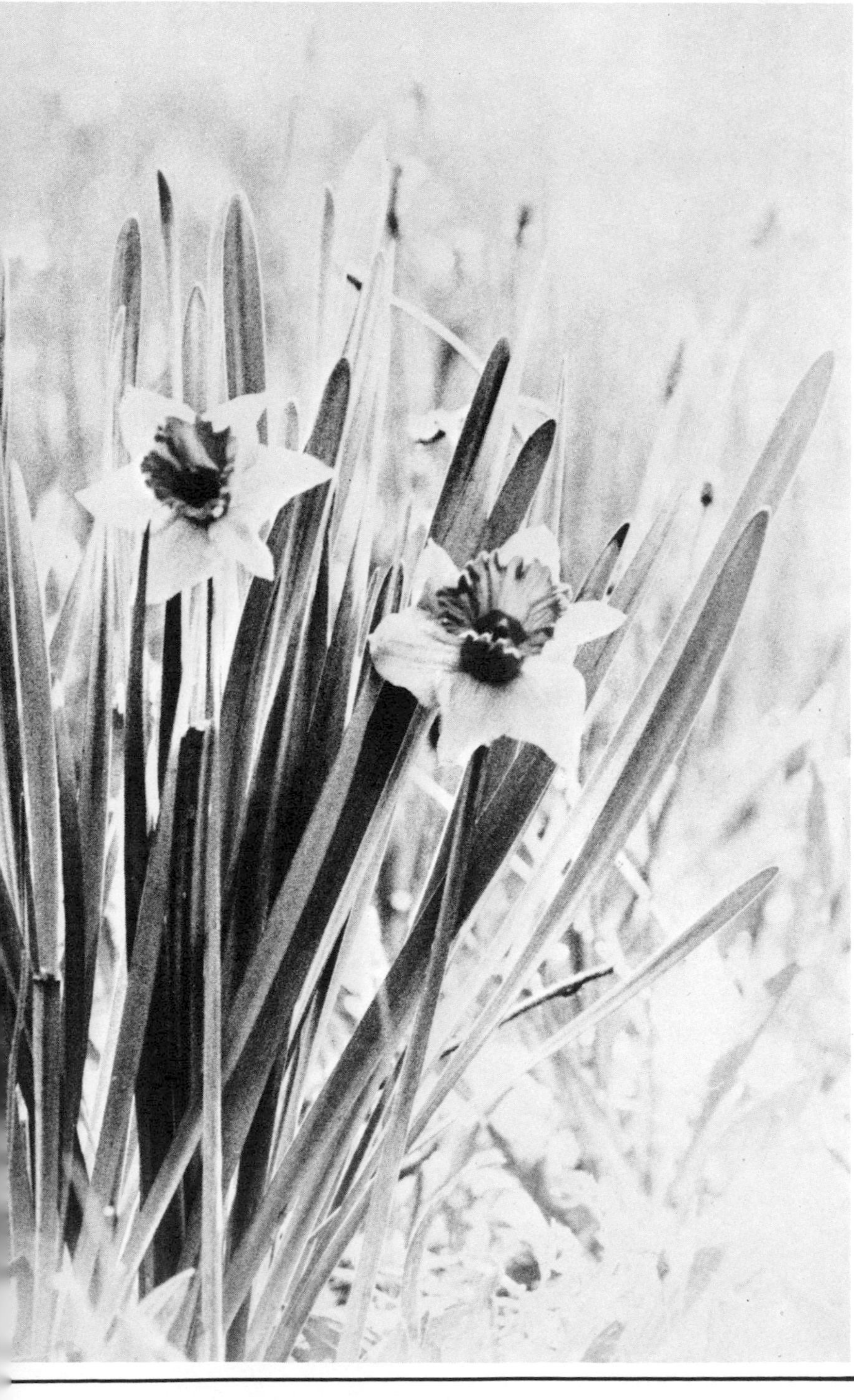

My life is turning around . . .
I don't know where it's going.
It's not going backwards
but sometimes I'm a little afraid,
sometimes I want to run . . .
but to where?

I'm concerned for you . . .
    I want to help
        but there seems to be nothing
I can do.

You have so much inside
and I know
        that in time
        things will be right
                for you again.
It just takes time . . .

So where do we go from here?

What happens to the love
    we've shared,
        the times we've been together,
          memories we've created?
Does it all fade away,
   blur together in a
      vague but pleasant
        recollection of something
that once was,
    but can never be again?

Can we keep it alive?

If I hurt you
it's not intentionally.
If you feel insecure with me
       it's not because I want it that way.
If I neglect to show you
how much I appreciate you,
   it's from a lack of awareness.
I try to do the best I can
but sometimes, in my bumbling,
           imperfect way,
I mess things up.
       Can you hear me?

I have been lonely
   and even your love
      could not cheer me.
No one could.
I was lonely
   for my own love.

How can people
  who love each other
so much
  cause such hurt
    for each other?

Why do I say things
    that hurt you?
Why do you get
  so upset?
Why do we always
    have to withdraw?
Can't you see I'm
  willing to let go of
    the hurt feelings
and be close?

Don't you know that
  all I really want
    is to love you?

As we sat together today, sharing,
a poem was growing in my mind.

You are my friend
and I want to give you something,
    a part of me.

How can I show you I care,
    or is it necessary? It's there—
        it can't be defined, or even described,
        Or destroyed.

Take my gift.
My friendship is what I have to give
you.
And in the taking, you'll be giving.

There's something special about you,
some indefinable extra
that makes . . . you.
It's what makes me keep on
loving you . . .
hoping my clumsy words
and childish moods
haven't destroyed
your love for me.
It's what keeps me going
when I know you're with
someone else, because
I know
that your heart
is still with me . . .

Night time.
Silence.
We are alone.
This time belongs to us
     as no other does.

Our bodies
     touching,
our voices
     silent,
our hearts
     together, peaceful
For a few hours
the world consists
     of you and me.

Morning comes
     and we slowly make our way
          back into the world
          of telephones
               and other people.

But it's all right
     because we always
     have
          our time.
The night belongs
                    to us.

Do I love you
       for what you are
       or what you give to me?
I hope it's just for
       what you are.
I'd like to think that
       you can be you
              and be free
                     to go your way
              whenever you need,
that there's nothing here
       to hold you to me
       but the gentle breeze
              that moves softly
                     between our souls,
and speaks the things
       our words could never express . . .

I reach out,
grasp,
struggle,
cry for help.
I am heard
but no one answers.
I am still alone,
listening
to myself.

I finally become aware
of you . . .
You are listening too,
silent,
alone.
There is a sadness
in your eyes
that I recognize . . .
I've felt it all too often
in my own.
We take a risk,
forget the pain
of our own sorrow.
At last, we are listening
to each other.

In our relationship
we have discovered
how much we have to strive
　　for our freedom . . .
not freedom from each other
　　but freedom with *each other,*
to be what we truly are
　　　　deep inside
and to know it's okay
　　to be
　　　　whatever that may be.

Midnight.
Waiting for you
to come home.
Soft-voiced nightsounds.
Heartbeat rhythm of crickets.
Gentle, cooling breeze.
Summer soon to be here.
Life slowing down,
    becoming easy,
        carefree,
    uncomplicated,
        dreamlike.
My mind is already there.
I wait for you
    to slow your life down
        and become carefree
            and easy too.
I want to help.
I hurt for you,
    seeing you unable
to step free of your commitments
and just take care of you.

Remember the time
    we spent together . . .
In a way those days
    will last forever.

Long after you
    and I have gone
the feelings we shared
        will linger on.

We traveled places far and near,
    we learned to love the land,
and grew to love ourselves as well,
            traveling hand in hand . . .

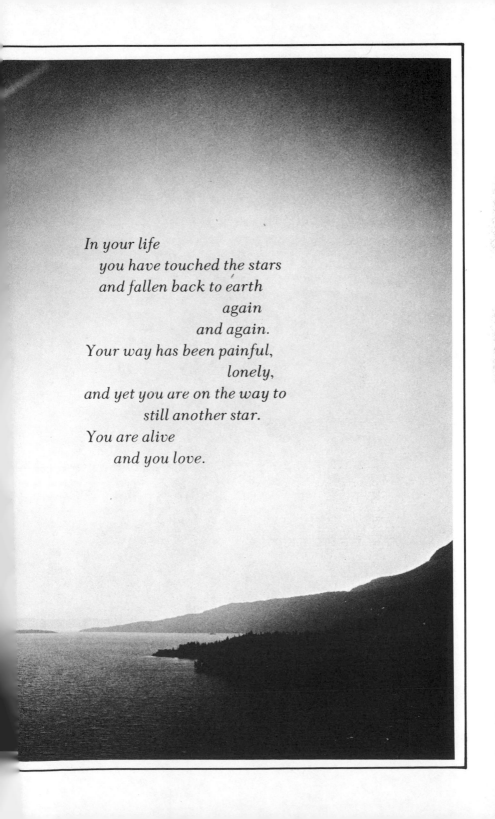

In your life
   you have touched the stars
   and fallen back to earth
                  again
               and again.
Your way has been painful,
                  lonely,
and yet you are on the way to
         still another star.
You are alive
   and you love.

We came together as strangers,
a little unsure
of what we wanted
and what we had to give.

One by one
*   strange faces became*
*   friendly ones*
*   and smiles were meant for us.*
The days passed quickly.
*   Friendship began to bloom*
*   and love gained new meaning.*
As we came to know a little
*   of each other,*
*   we grew to know more of*
*   who we are*
*   and what we can be.*

It's hard for me to take my leave
*   and accept that this has come*
*   to an end.*
But I take with me a new strength
and I leave behind a part of me
*   with each of you.*

I can not always be
beautiful
and unselfish.
You can not always be
kind
and understanding.
We are both human.
We have to be real.

I am so tired
but I want to stay awake
  all night
here in your arms
    so morning will seem
like a long time
          away.

It's not enough
for me today
to say "I love you."

I want to reach out
in a special way
and show you
how much
I care for you,
that I am here,
and to tell you
how much it means
to have you near,
knowing you love me.

You have become
   such a part of me
that I sometimes forget
      how important you are.
It means so much
   to know I am sharing
   my life with you.
We are
      developing
our own lives
      and building such
   a beautiful world together,
a world which has special meaning
      which only the two of us
            will share.

I lie here in bed
    listening to the clock
ticking away the seconds
    of the hours,
        of our lives.
And I realize how little time
        we have together . . .
Let us cherish it.

BOOKS OF RELATED INTEREST

A SHARED JOURNEY by Donni Betts is a journal recording her feelings, physically and emotionally, during the months of her pregnancy. She stresses the importance of the man being aware of and involved with the changes that take place while preparing for birth.
80 pages, soft cover, $3.95

GROWING TOGETHER by Donni and George Betts is the expression, in poetry, of a friendship that develops into love. A deep and moving tale of a relationship is enhanced by the beautiful photographs.
128 pages, soft cover, $3.95

VISIONS OF YOU by George Betts gives expression to the concerns of many. His poetry talks of everyone's yearnings and hopes and feelings. His voice is that of a friend, a lover, a person who cares.
128 pages, soft cover, $3.95

MY GIFT TO YOU by George Betts is his way of sharing a part of his life with the reader although they may never meet. To Betts sharing feelings is more important than knowing where we are from or where we are going.
128 pages, soft cover, $3.95

TEARS AND PEBBLES IN MY POCKET is George Betts sharing the times of struggle and the times of joy — both vital parts of growing. Betts's is a poetry of growth and awareness which awakens an understanding of our deepest feelings.
96 pages, soft cover, $3.95

FAREWELLS ARE ONLY BEGINNINGS by George Betts are poems of the ordinary, everyday events, the joys and sorrows we all experience. He helps us to understand and appreciate these experiences—to value them as a special gift.
96 pages, soft cover, $3.95

Available at your local book or department store or directly from the publisher. To order by mail, send check or money order to:

CELESTIAL ARTS
231 Adrian Road
Suite MPB
Millbrae, CA 94030

Please include $1.00 for postage and handling. California residents add 6% tax.